HMH

JOURNEYS

Write-In Reader

Grade 1 Vol. 1

Copyright © by Houghton Mifflin Harcourt Publishing Company

All rights reserved. No part of this work may be reproduced or transmitted in any form or by any means, electronic or mechanical, including photocopying or recording, or by any information storage and retrieval system, without the prior written permission of the copyright owner unless such copying is expressly permitted by federal copyright law. Requests for permission to make copies of any part of the work should be addressed to Houghton Mifflin Harcourt Publishing Company, Attn: Contracts, Copyrights, and Licensing, 9400 South Park Center Loop, Orlando, Florida 32819.

Printed in the U.S.A.

ISBN 978-0-547-87418-0

25 26 27 28 29 1468   21 20 19 18 17

4500669158   A B C D E F G

If you have received these materials as examination copies free of charge, Houghton Mifflin Harcourt Publishing Company retains title to the materials and they may not be resold. Resale of examination copies is strictly prohibited.

Possession of this publication in print format does not entitle users to convert this publication, or any portion of it, into electronic format.

Be a Reading Detective!

A detective looks for clues. You can look for clues, too. You can be a Reading Detective.

When you read, think about these questions:

▶ **Who?**

▶ **Where?**

▶ **When?**

▶ **What?**

▶ **Why?**

Look for clues to help you answer the questions.

"Let's try it! Follow the trail . . ."

Read the story. Think about these questions:

Who?   **Where?**   **When?**

> Marco and Papa are at the beach. It is sunny and hot. Papa hums a tune.
>
> "This is a great birthday!" Marco says.
>
> "Look, Marco!" Papa says. "Look at that!"

Answer the questions.

 Who is the story about?

 Where does the story take place?

3 When does the story take place?

Can you find clues to help you? If you can, you are a Reading Detective!

Contents

Unit 1

Lesson 1. 2

Pam and Fan 5

Lesson 2. 12

Pip Can Help 15

Lesson 3. 22

Bad Cat 25

Lesson 4 32

Dex 35

Lesson 5. 42

Sal 45

Unit 2

Lesson 6 52

Run, Run, Run! 55

Lesson 7. 62

Tell Cat! 65

Lesson 8. 72

Hit It! 75

Lesson 9 82

Scott and His Red Pen 85

Lesson 10 92

Who Can Help Cat? 95

Lesson 11 102

Pup's Bath 105

Lesson 12 112

Al and Lop 115

Lesson 13 122

Max Has His Bath 125

Lesson 14 132

Jake's Best Race 135

Lesson 15 142

Cats 145

Unit 3

My Pals

and
be
help
play

Read the sentence.
Write the new word.

1 Cat-cat can **play**.

play

2 Dan can **be** mad at Tad.

be

Copyright © by Houghton Mifflin Harcourt Publishing Company. All rights reserved.

3 Nan can **help** Dad.

help

4 Sam, Cam, **and** Tam sat.

and

Read the words in the word box.
Write the word under the picture.

mad	cat
mat	dad

1

2

3

4

Pam and Fan

by Emma Riba

Mad, mad, mad!

Copyright © by Houghton Mifflin Harcourt Publishing Company. All rights reserved.

Mad, mad, mad, mad!

Copyright © by Houghton Mifflin Harcourt Publishing Company. All rights reserved.

Pam can **be** mad, mad, mad.

Fan is sad.
Sad, sad, sad!

Copyright © by Houghton Mifflin Harcourt Publishing Company. All rights reserved.

Can Pam help Fan?
Can Fan help Pam?

Pam and Fan can!

Pam and Fan can play.

Check the answer.

1 Who is Pam?

☐ a girl   ☐ a dog

2 How is Pam feeling at first?

☐ sad   ☐ mad

3 What do Pam and Fan do?

☐ play   ☐ nap

Write about Pam.

_____

- -

4 Pam is _____.

Copyright © by Houghton Mifflin Harcourt Publishing Company. All rights reserved.

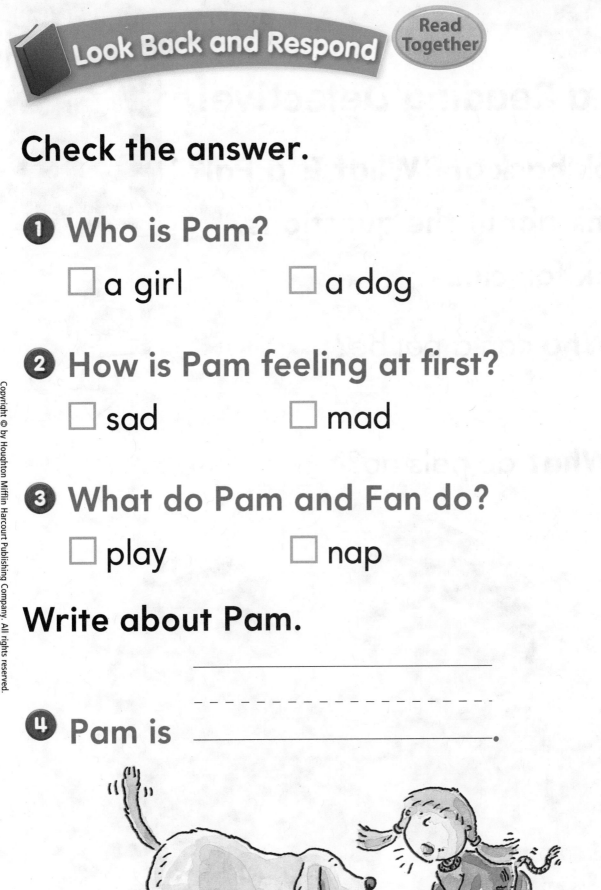

Be a Reading Detective!

"What Is a Pal?"
Student Book pp. 15–25

Look back at "What Is a Pal?"
Think about the questions.
Look for clues.

1 **Who** can a pal be?

2 **What** do pals do?

Write or draw your answer.

1 **Who** can a pal be?

Copyright © by Houghton Mifflin Harcourt Publishing Company. All rights reserved.

Talk about question 2.
Tell about the clues you found.

2 **What** do pals do?

Lesson

2

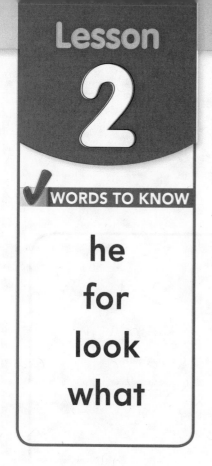

✓ WORDS TO KNOW

he
for
look
what

Weather

Read the sentence.
Write the new word.

1 Is **he** mad?

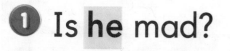

2 Did Pam **look** at it?

12

3 It is sad **for** Mip.

for

Copyright © by Houghton Mifflin Harcourt Publishing Company. All rights reserved.

4 Tap, tap, tap! See **what** it is.

what

Read the words in the word box.
Write the word under the picture.

pin	pit
tip	fin

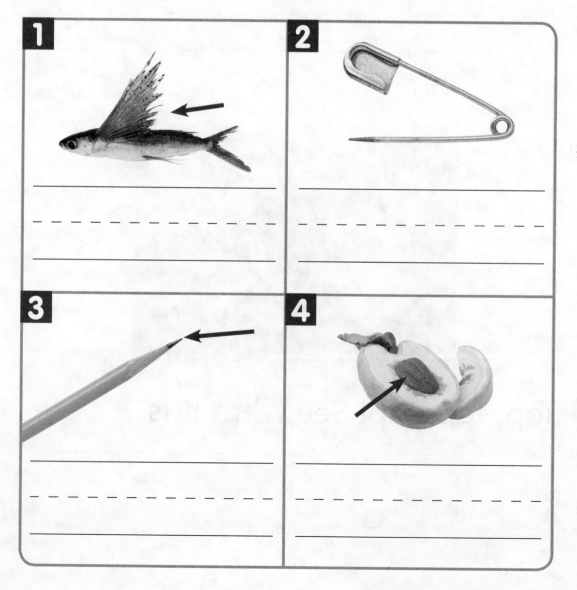

1.

2.

3.

4.

Mag   Big Sis   Dad   Tim   Pip

Pip Can Help

by Janice Winfield

Copyright © by Houghton Mifflin Harcourt Publishing Company. All rights reserved.

RIP, RAP, BAM!

Mag hid.

Big Sis ran in.

Copyright © by Houghton Mifflin Harcourt Publishing Company. All rights reserved.

Bam, bam, bam!
Dad ran in.

Dad sat with Mag.
Mag had a sip.

Copyright © by Houghton Mifflin Harcourt Publishing Company. All rights reserved.

Bam! Bam!

Tim ran in.

Look **what** Tim had **for** Mag.

He had Pip for Mag!

Pip can help Mag.

Zzzzzz.

Check the answer.

1 **Who hid?**

☐ Big Sis   ☐ Mag

2 **What did Dad give Mag?**

☐ a sip   ☐ a nap

3 **What did Tim have?**

☐ a nap   ☐ Pip

Write about a storm.

_____

4 **A storm is** _____.

Copyright © by Houghton Mifflin Harcourt Publishing Company. All rights reserved.

Be a Reading Detective!

Look back at "The Storm."
Think about the questions.
Look for clues.

Return to

"The Storm"
Student Book pp. 43–53

① **Who** is in the story?

② **What** happens?

Write or draw your answer.

1 **Who** is in the story?

Copyright © by Houghton Mifflin Harcourt Publishing Company. All rights reserved.

Talk about question 2.
Tell about the clues you found.

2 **What** happens?

do
funny
no
they

At School

Read the sentence.
Write the new word.

1 Sal had **no** bag.

no

2 Lib can **do** it!

do

3 It is not bad.

Can **they** can fix it?

they

4 His pal Rob is **funny**.

funny

Copyright © by Houghton Mifflin Harcourt Publishing Company. All rights reserved.

Read the words in the word box.
Write the word under the picture.

dot	log
mop	top

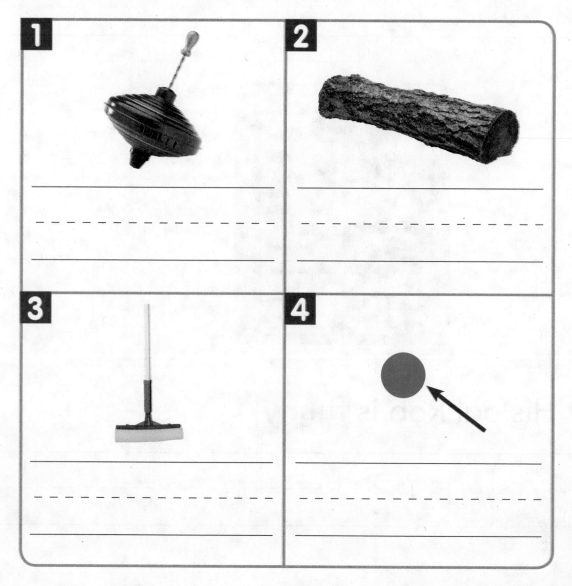

1

2

3

4

Bad Cat

by Marvin Hampton

Copyright © by Houghton Mifflin Harcourt Publishing Company. All rights reserved.

Dot is a **funny** cat.

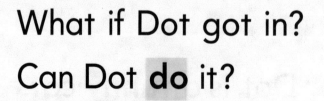

What if Dot got in?

Can Dot **do** it?

Copyright © by Houghton Mifflin Harcourt Publishing Company. All rights reserved.

Dot did it!

Dot got in.

Dot ran.

Dot ran on.

Copyright © by Houghton Mifflin Harcourt Publishing Company. All rights reserved.

Got him!

Can cats go in?

No, **they** can not!

30

Look Back and Respond

Check the answer.

1 **Where is Dot?**

☐ at school

☐ at home

2 **What happened first?**

☐ Dot got in.

☐ Dot ran on a hot pot.

3 **What happened last?**

☐ A lady said, "Cat!"

☐ A teacher got Dot.

Write about Dot.

4 Dot is _____.

Copyright © by Houghton Mifflin Harcourt Publishing Company. All rights reserved.

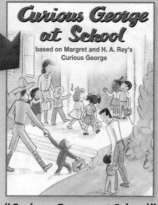

Return to

Curious George at School
based on Margret and H. A. Rey's
Curious George

"Curious George at School"
Student Book pp. 71–81

Be a Reading Detective!

Look back at "Curious George at School."

Think about the questions.

Look for clues.

1 Where is George?

2 What does George do?

Write or draw your answer.

1 **Where** is George?

Talk about question 2.
Tell about the clues you found.

2 **What** does George do?

Copyright © by Houghton Mifflin Harcourt Publishing Company. All rights reserved.

✓ **WORDS TO KNOW**

all

does

here

who

My Neighbors

Read the sentence.

Write the new word.

1 Pals can **all** fit on top.

all

2 Meg met Lin **here**.

here

Copyright © by Houghton Mifflin Harcourt Publishing Company. All rights reserved.

3 Big Ben **does** not let Ted win.

does

4 I see **who** it is!

who

Read the words in the word box.
Write the word under the picture.

| hen | red |
| ten | bed |

Dex

by Roberto Gómez

Copyright © by Houghton Mifflin Harcourt Publishing Company. All rights reserved.

It is big **here**.

Dex **does** not fit in.

Who can help Dex?

Hens can not.

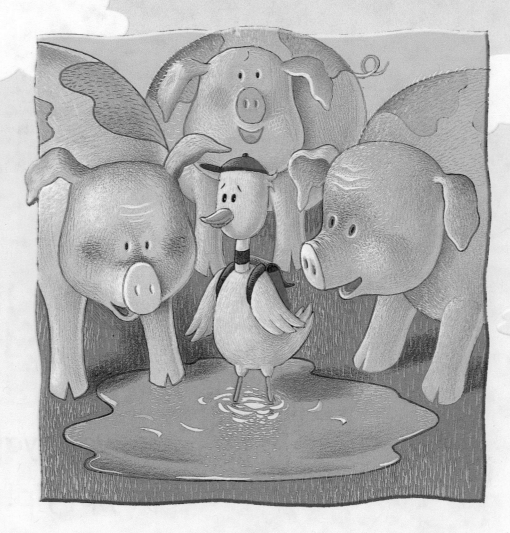

Copyright © by Houghton Mifflin Harcourt Publishing Company. All rights reserved.

Pigs can not.

Dex is not a pig.

Dogs can not.
All the dogs yap at him.

Copyright © by Houghton Mifflin Harcourt Publishing Company. All rights reserved.

Dex met Len.

Len led him here.

 It is not bad here.

It is not bad at all!

Look Back and Respond

Read Together

Check the answer.

1 **How do you know Dex is a duck?**

☐ from the words

☐ from the picture

2 **Where is the title?**

☐ on the first page

☐ on the last page

3 **On page 38, which dog is yapping?**

☐ the brown dog

☐ the gray dog

Write about Dex's home.

4 His home is _____.

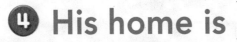

Copyright © by Houghton Mifflin Harcourt Publishing Company. All rights reserved.

Be a Reading Detective!

Look back at "Lucia's Neighborhood."
Think about the questions.
Look for clues.

Return to

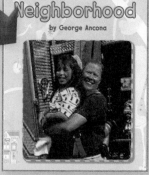

"Lucia's Neighborhood"
Student Book pp. 99–109

1 **Where** does Lucia go?

2 **What** does Lucia see?

Write or draw your answer.

1 **Where** does Lucia go?

Copyright © by Houghton Mifflin Harcourt Publishing Company. All rights reserved.

Talk about question 2.
Tell about the clues you found.

2 **What** does Lucia see?

friend

good

hold

many

At the Zoo

Read the sentence.

Write the new word.

1 The big cat runs with **many** cubs.

many

2 Yum, yum, yum! It is **good**!

good

3 His **friend** has bugs on him.

friend

Copyright © by Houghton Mifflin Harcourt Publishing Company. All rights reserved.

4 The pen can **hold** a big pig.

hold

Read the words in the word box.
Write the word under the picture.

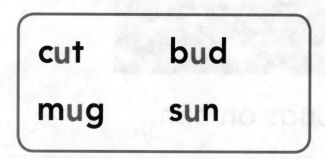

cut   bud

mug   sun

1

2

3

4

Sal

by Paola Rizzi

Sal begs for a pet.

His mom had **many** pets.

His mom is not a fan.

Copyright © by Houghton Mifflin Harcourt Publishing Company. All rights reserved.

Sal runs in.
Fun, fun, fun!

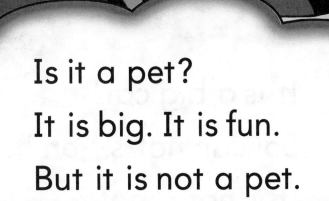

Copyright © by Houghton Mifflin Harcourt Publishing Company. All rights reserved.

Is it a pet?

It is big. It is fun.

But it is not a pet.

It is a big cat!
Sal can not sit on it.
It is not a pet.

Copyright © by Houghton Mifflin Harcourt Publishing Company. All rights reserved.

It is a big cub!

It can hug Sal.

No cub hugs for Sal!

Dad has a box.

What did it **hold**?

It is not a big cub.

But it is a **good friend**!

Look Back and Respond

Read Together

Check the answer.

1 **What does Sal want?**

☐ a pet

☐ a sister

2 **Where did Sal go?**

☐ to the vet

☐ to the zoo

3 **Who went with Sal?**

☐ his mom

☐ his dad

Write about an animal Sal saw.

4 _____

Copyright © by Houghton Mifflin Harcourt Publishing Company. All rights reserved.

Return to

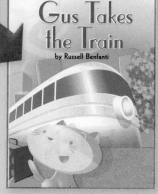

"Gus Takes the Train"
Student Book pp. 127–137

Be a Reading Detective!

Look back at "Gus Takes the Train."

Think about the questions.

Look for clues.

1 **Who** is in the story?

2 **Where** does Gus go?

Write or draw your answer.

1 **Who** is in the story?

Talk about question 2.
Tell about the clues you found.

2 **Where** does Gus go?

Copyright © by Houghton Mifflin Harcourt Publishing Company. All rights reserved.

away
come
every
said

Story Time

Read the sentence.
Write the new word.

1 Run, Miss!
Run **away**!

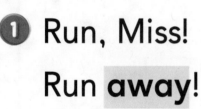

away

2 Who will **come** to fix him?

come

3 "It is big!" **said** Pig.

"It is bad!"

said

4 Jack and Jill go up **every** hill.

every

Copyright © by Houghton Mifflin Harcourt Publishing Company. All rights reserved.

Read the words in the word box.
Write the word under the picture.

sock   kiss

bell   egg

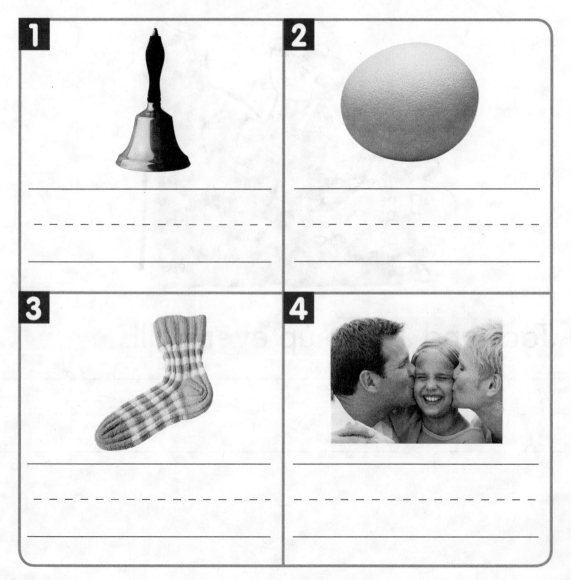

1

2

3

4

Run, Run, Run!

Tom

Jack

by Edith Rivera

Tom got set.

Jack got set.

Run, Tom! Run, Jack!

Run, run, run!

Copyright © by Houghton Mifflin Harcourt Publishing Company. All rights reserved.

Away Jack ran.

"I am quick," **said** Jack.

"I will win!"

Copyright © by Houghton Mifflin Harcourt Publishing Company. All rights reserved.

"**Come** on!" said Tom.

"Huff, huff, puff.

I will jog up **every** hill.

I will pass him yet!"

"Tom is not quick," said Jack.
"I can win in a jiff."

Copyright © by Houghton Mifflin Harcourt Publishing Company. All rights reserved.

Jack sat. Jack had a nap.

As Jack sat, Tom ran up.

"Rats!" said Jack. "Bad luck!"

"It is not luck," said Tom.

"I am not quick, but I did not quit!"

Check the answer.

1 **Who is Jack?**

☐ a bunny ☐ a turtle

2 **Is Jack quick?**

☐ yes ☐ no

3 **Why did Tom win?**

☐ Tom is quick.

☐ Tom did not quit.

Do you like Jack? Tell why.

_____

4 -

_____

Copyright © by Houghton Mifflin Harcourt Publishing Company. All rights reserved.

Be a Reading Detective!

Return to

"Jack and the Wolf"
Student Book pp. 15–29

Look back at "Jack and the Wolf."

Think about the questions.

Look for clues.

① **Who** is in the story?

② **What** happens?

Write or draw your answer.

① Who is in the story?

Copyright © by Houghton Mifflin Harcourt Publishing Company. All rights reserved.

Talk about question 2.
Tell about the clues you found.

② What happens?

animal

make

of

why

How Do Animals Talk?

Read the sentence.

Write the new word.

1 An **animal** can tell us if it is mad.

animal

2 Can you tell **why** it puffs up?

why

Copyright © by Houghton Mifflin Harcourt Publishing Company. All rights reserved.

3 Lots **of** ducks quack.

of

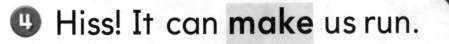

4 Hiss! It can **make** us run.

make

Read the words in the word box.
Write the word under the picture.

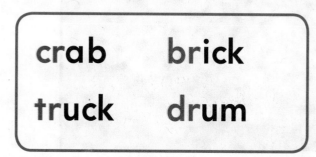

crab	brick
truck	drum

1

_____

- - - - - - - - - - -

_____

2

_____

- - - - - - - - - - -

_____

3

_____

- - - - - - - - - - -

_____

4

_____

- - - - - - - - - - -

_____

Tell Cat!

by Megan Linke

Copyright © by Houghton Mifflin Harcourt Publishing Company. All rights reserved.

"Quack, quack, quack," said Duck.
"Quack, quack! Quack, quack!"
But Cat did not see **why**.

"Crick, crick, crick," said Bug.

"Crick, crick! Crick, crick!"

"Hum?" said Cat.

Copyright © by Houghton Mifflin Harcourt Publishing Company. All rights reserved.

"Bick, bick, bick," said Pig.

"Bick, bick! Bick, bick!"

"Lots **of** mud!" said Cat.

"Pigs can **make** a mess."

"Grup, grup, grup," said Frog.

"Grup, grup! Grup, grup!"

"Frog is an odd **animal**," said Cat.

Copyright © by Houghton Mifflin Harcourt Publishing Company. All rights reserved.

"Buzz, buzz, buzz," I said.
"Buzz, buzz! Buzz, buzz!"

"Ack!" said Cat. "It is wet, wet, wet!"

Well, we did tell him!

But he did not get it.

Check the answer.

1 Who said "Grup, grup"?

☐ Duck   ☐ Frog

2 What are the animals telling Cat?

☐ where to get food

☐ that it may rain

3 Look at page 69.

What detail tells you it will rain?

☐ Cat   ☐ the clouds

Write about animal sounds.

4 What sound does a cat make?

_____

- -

_____

Copyright © by Houghton Mifflin Harcourt Publishing Company. All rights reserved.

Be a Reading Detective!

Look back at "How Animals Communicate."
Think about the questions.
Look for clues.

"How Animals Communicate"
by William Muñoz

"How Animals Communicate"
Student Book pp. 47–61

1 **How** do animals move?

2 **Why** do animals make sounds?

Write or draw your answer.

1 **How** do animals move?

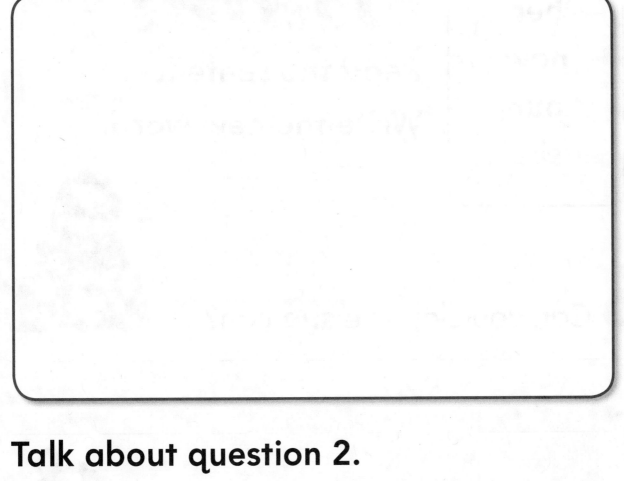

Talk about question 2.
Tell about the clues you found.

2 **Why** do animals make sounds?

Copyright © by Houghton Mifflin Harcourt Publishing Company. All rights reserved.

✓ WORDS TO KNOW

her

now

our

she

Music Time!

Read the sentence.

Write the new word.

1 Can you clap like **she** can?

she

2 Glenn will pick up his bell **now**.

now

3 Rat-tat-tat!

Jan slaps **her** drum.

her

4 Miss Glass tells **our** class to "hit it"!

our

Copyright © by Houghton Mifflin Harcourt Publishing Company. All rights reserved.

Read the words in the word box.
Write the word under the picture.

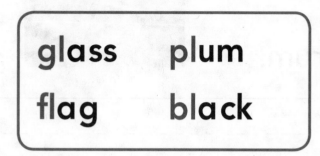

glass   plum

flag   black

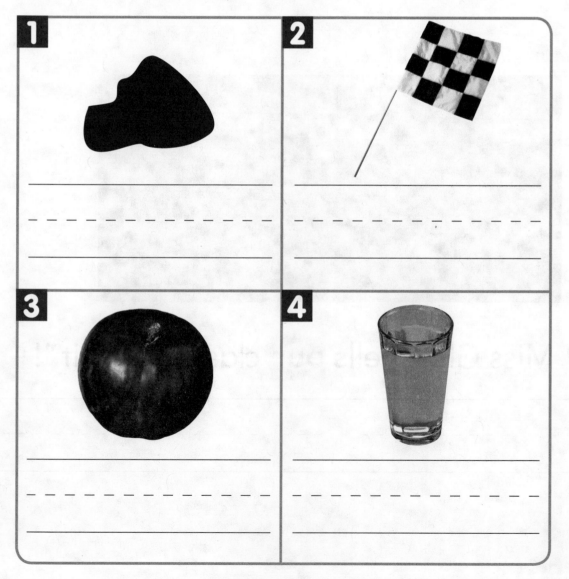

1

_____

- - - - - - - - - - - -

_____

2

_____

- - - - - - - - - - - -

_____

3

_____

- - - - - - - - - - - -

_____

4

_____

- - - - - - - - - - - -

_____

Pig   Duck   Hess   Frog   El

Hit It!

by Megan Linke

Copyright © by Houghton Mifflin Harcourt Publishing Company. All rights reserved.

Pig trots up.

Clip, clop, clip!

Now Duck hops in.
Duck puffs. **She** trills.

Copyright © by Houghton Mifflin Harcourt Publishing Company. All rights reserved.

Hess trots in back.

Clap, click! Click, clap!

Hess taps **her** drum.

Tat-tat! Pum-pum!

Our club is fun!

Plod! Clod! Crack!

Here is El. Ack!

Copyright © by Houghton Mifflin Harcourt Publishing Company. All rights reserved.

Not fun! Not fun!

Run, run, run!

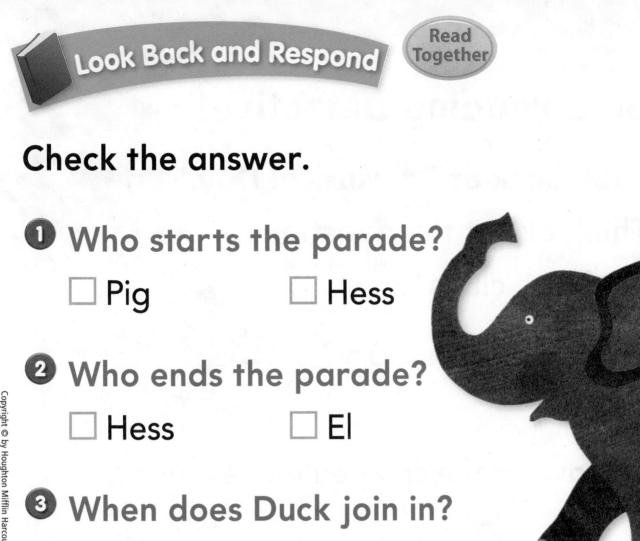

Check the answer.

1 Who starts the parade?

☐ Pig   ☐ Hess

2 Who ends the parade?

☐ Hess   ☐ El

3 When does Duck join in?

☐ after Hess   ☐ after Pig

Write about a parade you watched.

4 What did you see?

_____

— — — — — — — — — — — — — — — — — — — —

_____

Copyright © by Houghton Mifflin Harcourt Publishing Company. All rights reserved.

Return to
A Musical Day
by Jerdine Nolen
Illustrated by Frank Morrison

"A Musical Day"
Student Book pp. 79–93

Be a Reading Detective!

Look back at "A Musical Day."
Think about the questions.
Look for clues.

① **Who** is in the story?

② **How** do the children make music?

Write or draw your answer.

1 **Who** is in the story?

Copyright © by Houghton Mifflin Harcourt Publishing Company. All rights reserved.

Talk about question 2.
Tell about the clues you found.

2 **How** do the children make music?

✓ **WORDS TO KNOW**

after

read

was

write

Books and Writers

Read the sentence.
Write the new word.

1 Lib **was** in class.

was

2 Meg set it back **after** class.

after

82

Copyright © by Houghton Mifflin Harcourt Publishing Company. All rights reserved.

3 Skip can **read** to his sis.

read

4 Stan will **write** on his pad.

write

83

Write a Word

Read the words in the word box.
Write the word under the picture.

skull   step
stem   snack

1

_____

- - - - - - - - - - - -

_____

2

_____

- - - - - - - - - - - -

_____

3

_____

- - - - - - - - - - - -

_____

4

_____

- - - - - - - - - - - -

_____

Scott and His Red Pen

by Paolo Rizzi

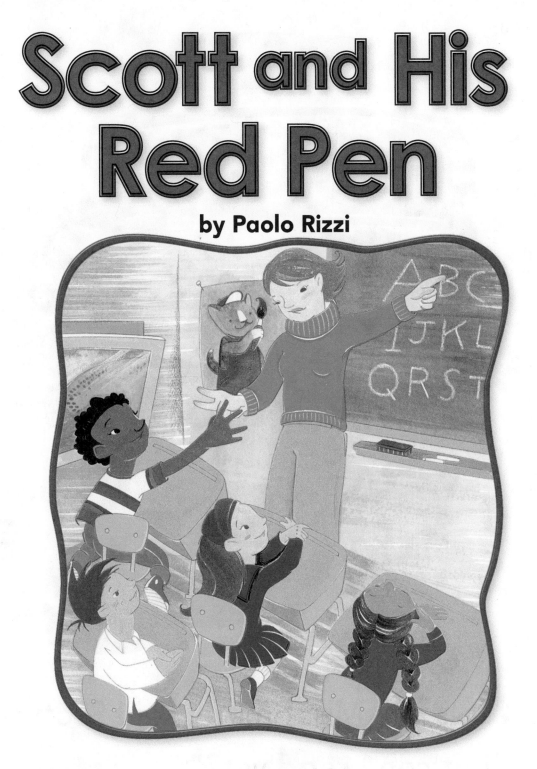

Scott sat in class.

Scott and his pals did the ABCs.

Copyright © by Houghton Mifflin Harcourt Publishing Company. All rights reserved.

"It is fun, Miss Smitt," said Scott.

"But can I **read** yet?"

"Not yet, Scott," said Miss Smitt.

"But you will!"

Copyright © by Houghton Mifflin Harcourt Publishing Company. All rights reserved.

It **was** not a snap.

But **after** a bit, Scott did it!

"It is fun, Dad," said Scott.

"But can I **write** yet?"

"Not yet, Scott," said his dad.

"But you will!"

Copyright © by Houghton Mifflin Harcourt Publishing Company. All rights reserved.

Scott had his pad.

Scott had his red pen.

Scott had big plans, as well.

Today, Scott is a man.
Scott still has his red pen.
Scott is a big hit!

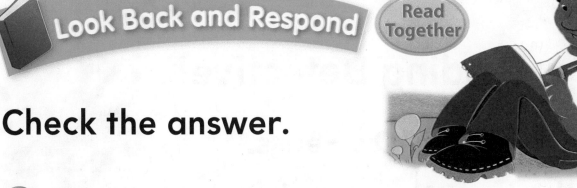

Look Back and Respond

Read Together

Check the answer.

1 Why is "ABC" on page 85?

☐ to teach us our ABCs

☐ to show what Scott is learning

2 What is this story called?

☐ Scott and His Red Pen

☐ Scott

3 Look at page 88. Where is Scott?

☐ at the library

☐ at home

Write about a book you like.

_____

4 _____

Copyright © by Houghton Mifflin Harcourt Publishing Company. All rights reserved.

Return to

Dr. Seuss
by Helen Lester

"Dr. Seuss"
Student Book pp. 111–125

Be a Reading Detective!

Look back at "Dr. Seuss."
Think about the questions.
Look for clues.

1 **What** did Dr. Seuss do?

2 **Who** likes Dr. Seuss?

Write or draw your answer.

1 **What** did Dr. Seuss do?

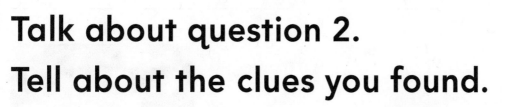

Talk about question 2.

Tell about the clues you found.

2 **Who** likes Dr. Seuss?

Copyright © by Houghton Mifflin Harcourt Publishing Company. All rights reserved.

Lesson 10

✓ WORDS TO KNOW

eat

give

put

take

Make It, Bake It!

Read the sentence.

Write the new word.

1 Ben will **put** milk in it.

put

2 Liz can **give** Grant a hand.

give

92

Copyright © by Houghton Mifflin Harcourt Publishing Company. All rights reserved.

3 Dad will **take** it if it is not too hot.

take

4 If Mom cuts it, Jan can help **eat** it!

eat

Read the words in the word box.
Write the word under the picture.

hand   plant
lamp   milk

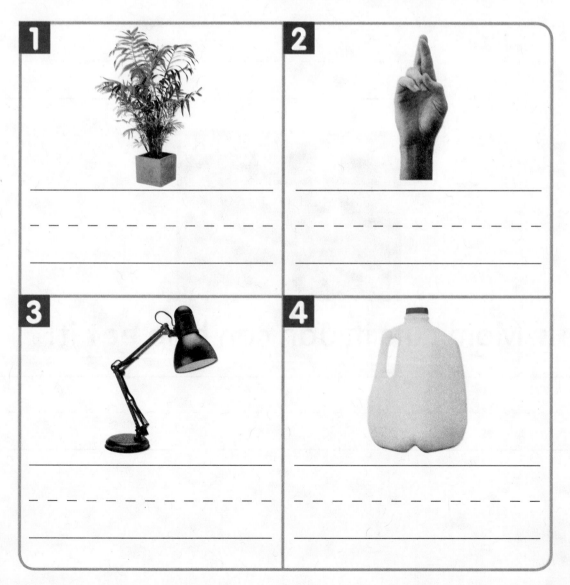

1

2

3

4

Cat   Kid   Hen   Don   Ness   Pig

Who Can Help Cat?

by Marc Vargas

Cat has a plan.

Who can help?

Copyright © by Houghton Mifflin Harcourt Publishing Company. All rights reserved.

Kid can help Cat!
Kid will mix it up.

Copyright © by Houghton Mifflin Harcourt Publishing Company. All rights reserved.

Don will fix the crust.

Don will **take** it and press it flat.

Ness can help, too.
Ness will **put** it in a pan.

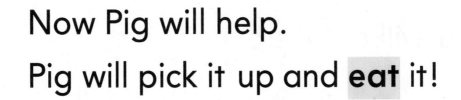

Copyright © by Houghton Mifflin Harcourt Publishing Company. All rights reserved.

Now Pig will help.

Pig will pick it up and **eat** it!

No, Pig!

Cat will cut it up.

And Cat will **give** a bit to all of us!

Check the answer.

1 Where does the story take place?

☐ a kitchen   ☐ a bedroom

2 Who wants help?

☐ Hen   ☐ Cat

3 What does Pig try to do?

☐ eat the pie   ☐ help Cat

Write about the story.

_____

- - - - - - - - - - - - - - - - -

4 Who helps Cat? _____

Copyright © by Houghton Mifflin Harcourt Publishing Company. All rights reserved.

Return to

A Cupcake Party
written and illustrated by
David McPhail

"A Cupcake Party"
Student Book pp. 143–157

Be a Reading Detective!

Look back at "A Cupcake Party."

Think about the questions.

Look for clues.

① **Who** is in the story?

② **What** happens at Fritz's house?

Write or draw your answer.

1 **Who** is in the story?

Copyright © by Houghton Mifflin Harcourt Publishing Company. All rights reserved.

Talk about question 2.
Tell about the clues you found.

2 **What** happens at Fritz's house?

✓ **WORDS TO KNOW**

far
little
water
where

Sea Animals

Read the sentence.
Write the new word.

1 This **little** crab sits on its rock.

little

2 Gulls can nest **far** up on cliffs.

far

3 Can you tell **where** it is?

where

4 This **water** has lots in it!

water

Copyright © by Houghton Mifflin Harcourt Publishing Company. All rights reserved.

Read the words in the word box.
Write the word under the picture.

bath	math
moth	path

1

_____

- - - - - - - - -

_____

2

_____

- - - - - - - - -

_____

3

_____

- - - - - - - - -

_____

4

$$3$$
$$-\,2$$
$$\overline{1}$$

_____

- - - - - - - - -

_____

Pup's Bath

by Diane Bird

Copyright © by Houghton Mifflin Harcourt Publishing Company. All rights reserved.

Pup sat in his bath.

Mom sat with him.

"What is in this **water**?" asked Pup.

"Can you swim?" asked Mom.

Pup ducked.

Pup swam and swam.

Pup met lots of **little** pals.

Copyright © by Houghton Mifflin Harcourt Publishing Company. All rights reserved.

Then Pup swam up to a big grin!

"Ack!" yelped Pup.

"Mom! **Where** is my mom?"

But Mom was **far** away.
Pup swam up, up, up.

Copyright © by Houghton Mifflin Harcourt Publishing Company. All rights reserved.

Then Pup sat up.

"Mom!" yelled Pup.

"What a trip!"

Then his mom just picked him up.
"Off to bed," Mom said.

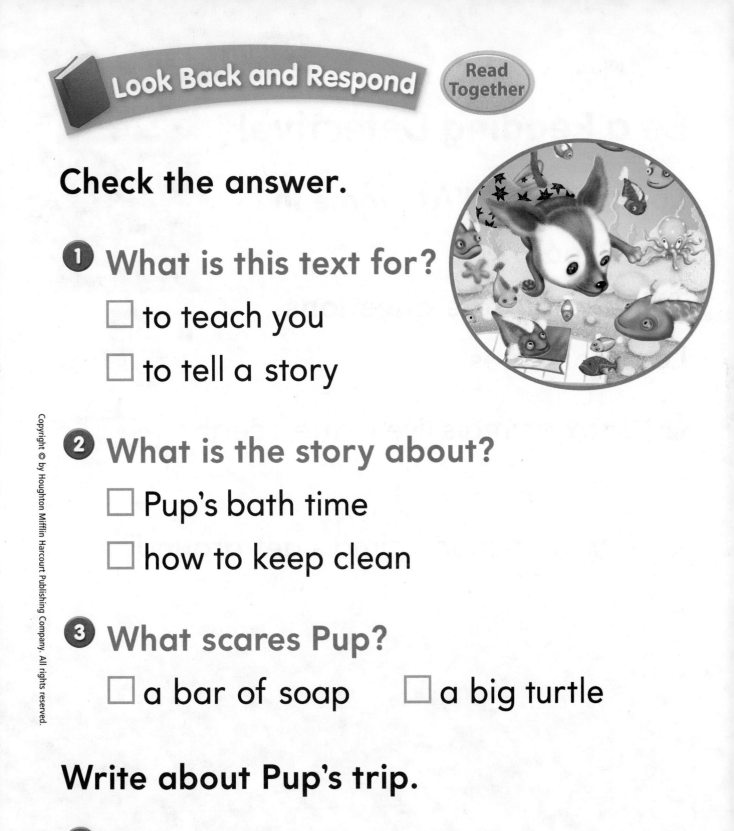

Check the answer.

1 **What is this text for?**

☐ to teach you

☐ to tell a story

2 **What is the story about?**

☐ Pup's bath time

☐ how to keep clean

3 **What scares Pup?**

☐ a bar of soap   ☐ a big turtle

Write about Pup's trip.

4 **What did he see?**

_____

_ _ _ _ _ _ _ _ _ _ _ _ _ _ _ _ _

_____

Copyright © by Houghton Mifflin Harcourt Publishing Company. All rights reserved.

 Return to

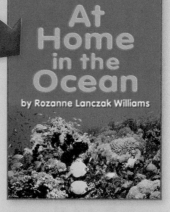 At Home in the Ocean

by Rozanne Lanczak Williams

"At Home in the Ocean"
Student Book pp. 15–29

Be a Reading Detective!

Look back at "At Home in the Ocean."

Think about the questions.

Look for clues.

① **What** animals live in the ocean?

② **How** do ocean animals get around?

Write or draw your answer.

1 **What** animals live in the ocean?

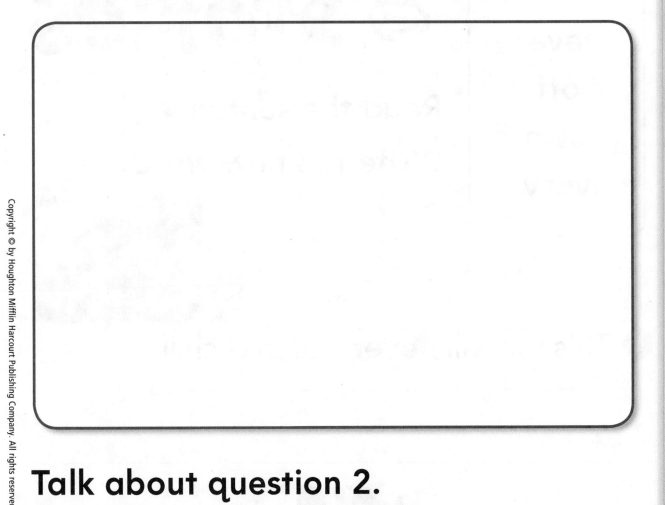

Talk about question 2.
Tell about the clues you found.

2 **How** do ocean animals get around?

Copyright © by Houghton Mifflin Harcourt Publishing Company. All rights reserved.

Animal Stories

Read the sentence.

Write the new word.

1 This fox will **never** catch a chill.

never

2 Hess has spots that will not rub **off**.

Copyright © by Houghton Mifflin Harcourt Publishing Company. All rights reserved.

3 A chick will stick with its **own** mom.

own

4 This animal can chop logs **very** well.

very

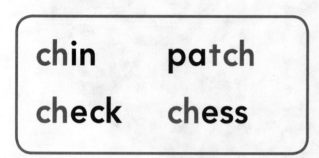
Read the words in the word box.
Write the word under the picture.

chin	patch
check	chess

1

_____

- - - - - - - - - -

_____

2

_____

- - - - - - - - - -

_____

3

_____

- - - - - - - - - -

_____

4

_____

- - - - - - - - - -

_____

Al and Lop

by Megan Linke

Copyright © by Houghton Mifflin Harcourt Publishing Company. All rights reserved.

This is Lop.

Lop did not like water **very** much.

But Lop had his tricks.

"Al!" yelled Lop.

"I have lots of pals!"

Copyright © by Houghton Mifflin Harcourt Publishing Company. All rights reserved.

"Not as many as I do!" yelled Al.

"Run and fetch them," yelled Lop.

"Then we will see!"

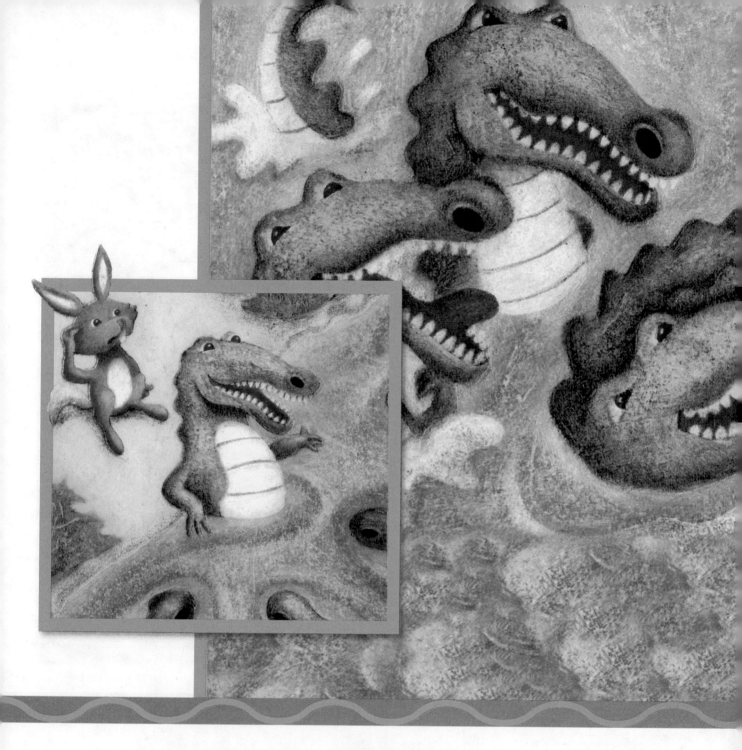

Al fetched his **own** pals.

But Lop just scratched his chin.

"This will **never** do!" clucked Lop.

"Set them up in a path."

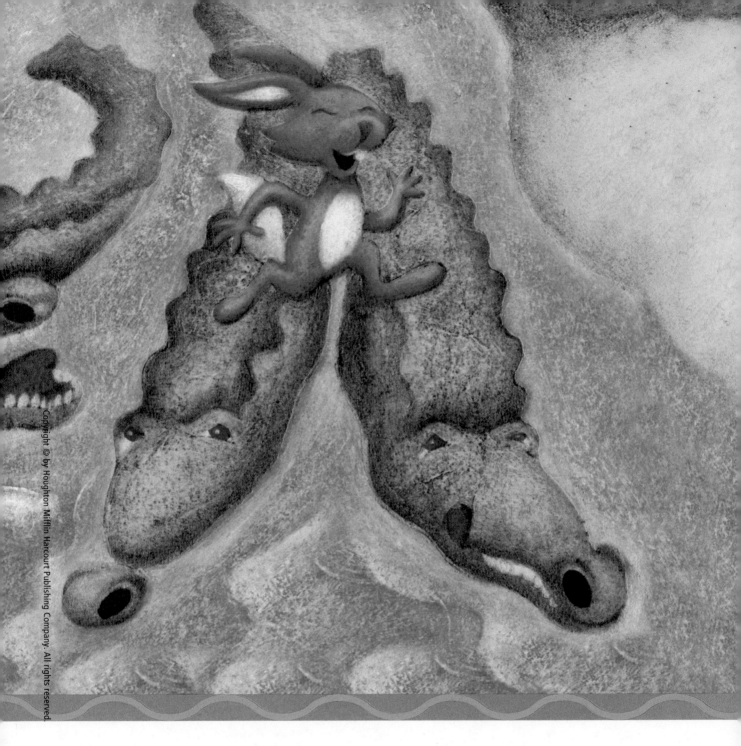

Copyright © by Houghton Mifflin Harcourt Publishing Company. All rights reserved.

Al did.

Hop, hop, hop!

Lop ran on top of them.

Al's pals got mad, mad, mad!

Chomp! Al bit Lop as he got **off**.

Now all Lop has left is a puff of fluff!

Look Back and Respond

Read Together

Check the answer.

1 Whom do we see first?

☐ Al   ☐ Lop

2 What happened last?

☐ Lop had to cross a river.

☐ Lop ran away.

3 What happened after Al's pals got mad?

☐ Al bit Lop.   ☐ Lop swam.

Write about the story.

4 Do you think Lop's trick was smart?

_____

- - - - - - - - - - - - - - - - - -

_____

Copyright © by Houghton Mifflin Harcourt Publishing Company. All rights reserved.

Return to

How
Leopard
Got His Spots
Gerald McDermott

"How Leopard Got His Spots"
Student Book pp. 47–63

Be a Reading Detective!

Look back at "How Leopard Got His Spots."

Think about the questions.

Look for clues.

1 **What** animals are in the story?

2 **How** did Leopard get his spots?

121A

Write or draw your answer.

1 **What** animals are in the story?

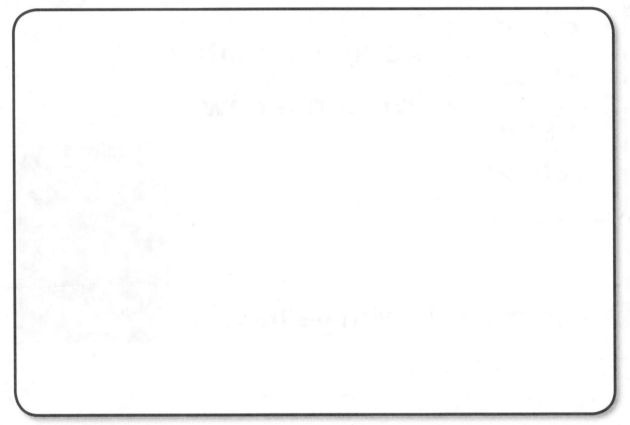

Talk about question 2.
Tell about the clues you found.

2 **How** did Leopard get his spots?

Copyright © by Houghton Mifflin Harcourt Publishing Company. All rights reserved.

✔ **WORDS TO KNOW**

down

goes

open

yellow

Seasons Changing

Read the sentence.
Write the new word.

1 Red mixes in with **yellow**.

yellow

2 Josh rushes **down** on his sled.

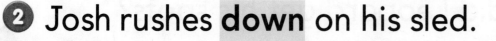

down

122

Copyright © by Houghton Mifflin Harcourt Publishing Company. All rights reserved.

3 Buds **open** up.

open

4 Ash **goes** shell hunting with Jen.

goes

Write a Word

Read the words in the word box.
Write the word under the picture.

dish	ship
shell	cash

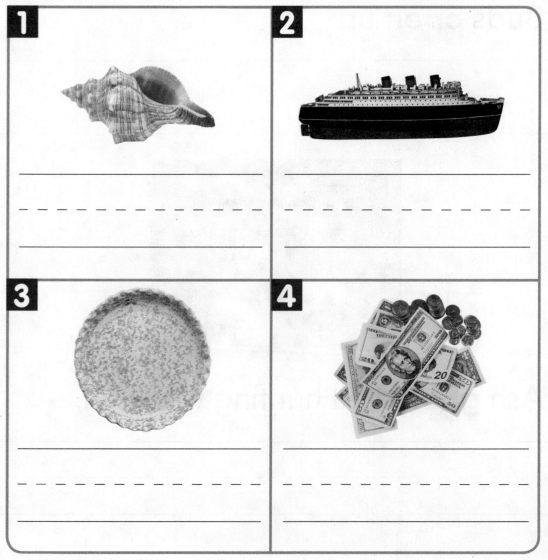

1

_____

- - - - - - - - - - - - -

_____

2

_____

- - - - - - - - - - - - -

_____

3

_____

- - - - - - - - - - - - -

_____

4

_____

- - - - - - - - - - - - -

_____

Max Has His Bath

by Emma Riba

© by Houghton Mifflin Harcourt Publishing Company. All rights reserved.

Water gushes **down**.

It fills our path with mud.

Max has such fun splashing in that mess!

Then Max has his bath.

Max does not wish to have his bath.

But he must.

Copyright © by Houghton Mifflin Harcourt Publishing Company. All rights reserved.

Now it is hot.

Max has **yellow** dust on him.

Phil pats his back.

Then Max **goes** in the tub!

In fall, twigs stick on Max.

I tell him, "Hop in, Max!"

But Max will not hop in.

I will pick him up and plop him in!

Copyright © by Houghton Mifflin Harcourt Publishing Company. All rights reserved.

Now it is cold.

Max stands out in the **open**.

Slush melts on his back.

Now I will not ask Max.

Phil will not ask him.

But in a flash, Max will rush in.

Max is all set for his hot bath!

Check the answer.

1 Why does Max have so many baths?

☐ He is always hot.

☐ He is always a mess.

2 Why does Big Sis pick Max up?

☐ He will not hop into the tub.

☐ He is cold.

3 What happens when Max is cold?

☐ He does not need a bath.

☐ He wants a bath.

Write about Max in winter.

_____

4 Max likes his _____.

Copyright © by Houghton Mifflin Harcourt Publishing Company. All rights reserved.

"Seasons"
Student Book pp. 81–99

Be a Reading Detective!

Look back at "Seasons."

Think about the questions.

Look for clues.

1 **What** happens in the spring?

2 **When** does the weather get colder?

Write or draw your answer.

① What happens in the spring?

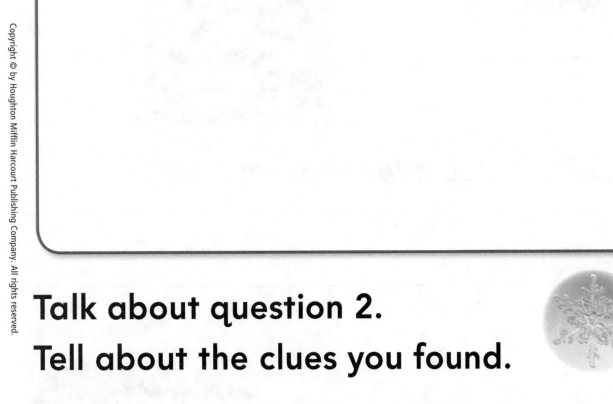

Talk about question 2.

Tell about the clues you found.

② When does the weather get colder?

Copyright © by Houghton Mifflin Harcourt Publishing Company. All rights reserved.

✓ **WORDS TO KNOW**

over

three

two

watch

Races

Read the sentence.

Write the new word.

1 Do not step **over** that tape yet!

over

2 Fans **watch** and clap.

watch

Copyright © by Houghton Mifflin Harcourt Publishing Company. All rights reserved.

3 The **three** kids hold eggs.

three

4 Ron held up his **two** hands.

two

Read the words in the word box.
Write the word under the picture.

snake	tape
plane	game

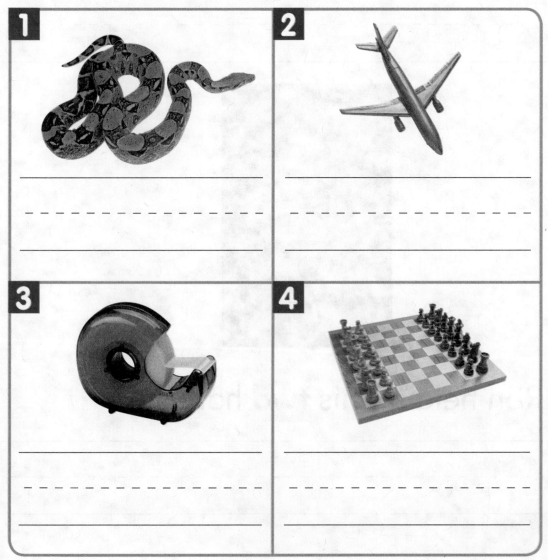

1

2

3

4

Jake's Best Race

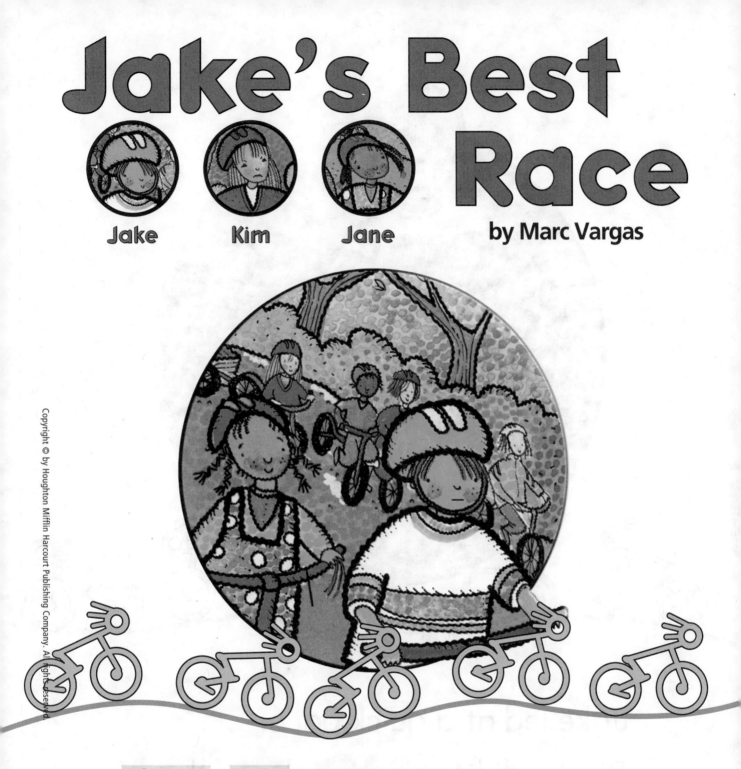

Jake   Kim   Jane

by Marc Vargas

Copyright © by Houghton Mifflin Harcourt Publishing Company. All Rights Reserved.

Three, **two**, one!

Jake shot off.

"I must win this race," hissed Jake.

"If not, it will not be fun."

Jake led at a quick pace.

But he did not **watch** the path.

Thump! Jake ran **over** a big rock.

Copyright © by Houghton Mifflin Harcourt Publishing Company. All rights reserved.

Bam! Jake fell.

As Jake sat, Kim ran up.

"Face it, Jake," said Kim.

"You will not race."

Then Kim ran off.

Copyright © by Houghton Mifflin Harcourt Publishing Company. All rights reserved.

As Kim left, Jane came up.

"My name is Jane," she said.

And she gave Jake a hand.

In the end, Jake did not win.

But he still had fun.

He had fun with his new pal, Jane.

Check the answer.

1 Why can't Jake race?

☐ because he fell

☐ because he had to go home

2 Why was this Jake's "best" race?

☐ because he won

☐ because he met Jane

3 What will happen next?

☐ Jake and Jane will be pals.

☐ Jake will finish the race.

Write about a race you were in.

_____

4 _____

_____

Copyright © by Houghton Mifflin Harcourt Publishing Company. All rights reserved.

Return to

The
Big Race
written by Pam Muñoz Ryan
illustrated by Viviana Garofoli

"The Big Race"
Student Book pp. 125–143

Be a Reading Detective!

Look back at "The Big Race."
Think about the questions.
Look for clues.

1 **Who** runs in the race?

2 **What** does Red Lizard do with his cake?

Write or draw your answer.

1 **Who** runs in the race?

Copyright © by Houghton Mifflin Harcourt Publishing Company. All rights reserved.

Talk about question 2.
Tell about the clues you found.

2 **What** does Red Lizard do with his cake?

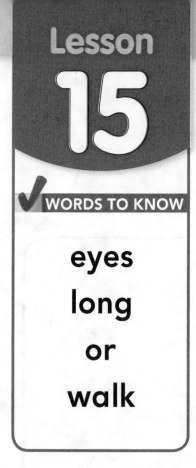

✓ **WORDS TO KNOW**

eyes

long

or

walk

Read the sentence.

Write the new word.

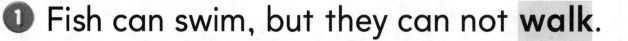

1 Fish can swim, but they can not **walk**.

walk

2 Snakes can eat mice **or** frogs.

or

Copyright © by Houghton Mifflin Harcourt Publishing Company. All rights reserved.

3 Bugs can have **long** legs.

long

4 A cat's quick **eyes** help it hunt.

eyes

Read the words in the word box.
Write the word under the picture.

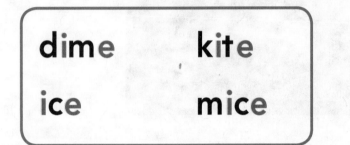

dime   kite

ice   mice

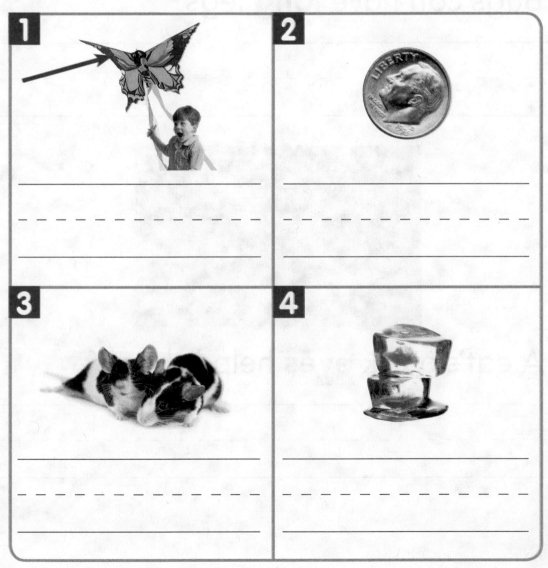

1

_____

- - - - - - - - -

_____

2

_____

- - - - - - - - -

_____

3

_____

- - - - - - - - -

_____

4

_____

- - - - - - - - -

_____

Cats

by Edith Rivera

Copyright © by Houghton Mifflin Harcourt Publishing Company. All rights reserved

Some say that cats have nine lives.

This is not the case.

But cats can still do a lot!

Cats can be big **or** small.
But all cats can bite. Yikes!

Copyright © by Houghton Mifflin Harcourt Publishing Company. All rights reserved.

This big cat is black with spots.

Its spots help it hide.

This cat sits on a **long** branch.

It has its **eyes** wide open.

If it spots an animal, it strikes!

This big cat hunts as well.
It can hunt mice, fish, and frogs.

Copyright © by Houghton Mifflin Harcourt Publishing Company. All rights reserved.

Big cats can look like pets.

But it is not wise to pet them!

Never **walk** up to big cats.

It is best just to let them be.

Check the answer.

1 How are all cats the same?

☐ They are the same size.

☐ They can all bite.

2 How can big cats differ?

☐ in color

☐ some have teeth, some don't

3 If you see a big cat...

☐ walk up to it.

☐ let it be.

Write about cats.

4 Cats are _____ .

Copyright © by Houghton Mifflin Harcourt Publishing Company. All rights reserved.

Animal Groups
by James Bruchac

Be a Reading Detective!

Look back at "Animal Groups."

Think about the questions.

Look for clues.

"Animal Groups"
Student Book pp. 165–183

1 **What** are mammals?

2 **How** are all fish the same?

Write or draw your answer.

1 **What** are mammals?

Talk about question 2.

Tell about the clues you found.

2 **How** are all fish the same?

Copyright © by Houghton Mifflin Harcourt Publishing Company. All rights reserved.

Summarize Strategy

You can **summarize** what you read.

• Tell important ideas in your own words.

• Tell ideas in an order that makes sense.

• Keep the meaning of the text.

• Use only a few sentences.

Analyze/Evaluate Strategy

You can **analyze** and **evaluate** a text. Think carefully about what you read. Form an opinion about it.

1. Think about the text and the author.
   - What are the important facts and ideas?
   - What does the author want you to know?

2. Decide what is important. Then form an opinion.
   - How do you feel about what you read?
   - Do you agree with the author's ideas?

Copyright © by Houghton Mifflin Harcourt Publishing Company. All rights reserved.

Infer/Predict Strategy

Use clues to figure out what the author does not tell you. Then you are making an **inference**.

Use clues to figure out what will happen next. Then you are making a **prediction**.

Monitor/Clarify Strategy

Monitor what you read. Make sure it makes sense.

Find a way to understand what does not.

• Reread.

• Read ahead.

• Ask questions.

Question Strategy

Ask yourself **questions** as you read.

Look for answers.

Some questions to ask:

- What does the author mean?
- Who or what is this about?
- Why did this happen?
- What is the main idea?

Visualize Strategy

You can **visualize**.

- Make pictures in your mind as you read.
- Use words in the text to help you.
- Make pictures of people, places, things, and actions.

Copyright © by Houghton Mifflin Harcourt Publishing Company. All rights reserved.

PHOTO CREDITS

Placement Key: (r) right, (l) left, (c) center, (t) top, (b) bottom, (bg) background

blind ii © Comstock/Getty Images. blind iii © nito/Fotolia. 2 (tr) © Shutterstock. 2 (b) © Rubberball Productions. 4 (tr) © PhotoDisc, Inc. 4 (bl) © Artville. 4 (tl) © PhotoDisc, Inc. 4 (br) © Rubberball Productions. 11A Tetra/Getty Images. 11B © PhotoDisc/Getty Images. 12 (t) © Getty Images/PhotoDisc. 12 (b) © Getty Images/PhotoDisc. 13 (t) © Corel Stock Photo Library. 13 (b) © Getty Images/PhotoDisc. 14 (tr) © PhotoDisc, Inc. 14 (tl) © Stockbyte. 14 (bl) © Photolink/PhotoDisc. 14 (br) © Image Club. 15 © Comstock. 17 © Classic PIO Images. 18 © PhotoDisc, Inc. 19 © Shutterstock. 21A © Houghton Mifflin Harcourt. 21B Comstock/Getty Images. 24 (tl) © PhotoDisc, Inc. 24 (tr) © PhotoDisc, Inc. 24 (bl) © Stockbyte. 31A © Houghton Mifflin Harcourt. 31B © Houghton Mifflin Harcourt. 32 (t) © Getty Images/PhotoDisc. 33 (t) © Superstock. 33 (b) © Getty Images/PhotoDisc. 34 (tl) © Getty Images/PhotoDisc. 34 (tr) © Shutterstock. 41A Stockbyte/Getty Images. 41A © Antenna Audio, Inc./Getty Images. 41B © Houghton Mifflin Harcourt. 42 (t) © Brand X Pictures. 42 (b) © Alamy. 43 (t) © Corel Stock Photo Library. 43 (b) © Digital Vision/Getty Images. 44 (tl) © PhotoDisc, Inc. 44 (tr) © PhotoDisc/Getty Images. 44 (br) © Eyewire/Getty Images. 51A © Corbis RF. 51B Mel Yates/Digital Vision/Getty Images. 54 (tl) © Artville. 54 (tr) © Getty Images/PhotoDisc. 54 (bl) © Brand X Pictures. 54 (br) © Digital Vision. 61A (b) © Houghton Mifflin Harcourt. 61B (b) © Carol Lee/Alamy Images. 62 (t) © Corel Stock Photo Library. 62 (b) © Photodisc, Inc. 63 (t) © Corel Stock Photo Library. 63 (b) © Corel Stock Photo Library. 64 (tl) © Getty Images/PhotoDisc. 64 (tr) © PhotoDisc, Inc. 64 (br) © Getty Images/PhotoDisc. 64 (bl) © PhotoDisc, Inc. 71A (b) © Getty Images. 71B (b) © steve greer/iStock. 74 (tr) © PhotoDisc, Inc. 74 (bl) © Artville. 74 (br) © Corbis. 81A (b) © Houghton Mifflin Harcourt. 81A (cr) © Ocean/Corbis. 81B (b) Stockbyte/Getty Images. 81B (b) © Tetra Images/Tetra Images/Corbis. 82 (t) © PhotoDisc, Inc. 84 (tl) © PhotoDisc/Getty Images. 84 (tr) © Artville. 84 (bl) © Getty Images/

PhotoDisc. 84 (br) © Getty Images/PhotoDisc. 91A (b) © Houghton Mifflin Harcourt. 91B (b) © Houghton Mifflin Harcourt. 94 (tl) © Siede Preis/PhotoDisc, Inc. 94 (tr) © PhotoDisc, Inc. 94 (bl) © PhotoDisc, Inc. 94 (br) © Ryan McVay/PhotoDisc, Inc. 95–100 (border) © PhotoDisc, Inc. 101A (b) © JGI/Jamie Grill/Getty Images. 101B (b) Getty Images/Photodisc. 102 (t) © Corel Stock Photo Library. 102 (b) © Stockbyte/Getty Images. 103 (t) © Getty Images/PhotoDisc. 103 (c) © Getty Images/PhotoDisc. 103 (b) © Getty Images/Digital Vision. 104 (tl) © Stockbyte. 104 (bl) © Digital Vision. 111A (b) © Westend61 GmbH/Alamy. 111B (b) © HMH. 112 (t) © Corbis. 112 (b) © Corbis. 113 (t) © Royalty Free/Corbis. 113 (b) © Corel Stock Photo Library. 114 (tl) © PhotoDisc/Getty Images. 114 (bl) © PhotoDisc, Inc. 114 (br) © Rubber Ball/Getty Images. 121A (b) © Comstock/Getty Images. 121B (b) Comstock/Getty Images. 122 (t) © Corbis. 122 (b) © Adobe Image Library. 123 (t) © Corbis. 123 (b) © Getty Images/PhotoDisc. 124 (tl) © Eyewire/Getty Images. 124 (tr) © Classic PIO Images. 124 (bl) © Digital Vision. 124 (br) © Masterfile. 131A (b) Getty Images Royalty Free. 131B (b) Comstock/Getty Images. 131B (b) © Cavan Images/Getty Images. 132 (t) © Bigshots/Getty Images. 132 (b) © Superstock. 133 (t) © Getty Images. 133 (b) © Corbis. 134 (tl) © PhotoDisc, Inc. 134 (tr) © PhotoDisc, Inc. 134 (bl) © Artville. 134 (br) © PhotoDisc, Inc. 141A (b) PhotoDisc/Getty Images. 141B (b) © Houghton Mifflin Harcourt. 142 (t) © Eyewire. 142 (b) © Photospin. 143 (t) © Corel Stock Photo Library. 143 (b) © Getty Images/PhotoDisc. 144 (tl) © Getty Images/Rubberball Productions. 144 (bl) © Shutterstock. 144 (br) © Alamy. 145 (t) © Getty Images. 145 (bl) © Shutterstock. 145 (border) © Getty Images/Digital Vision. 146–147 (border) © Getty Images/PhotoDisc. 146 (br) © Shutterstock. 148–149 (border) © PhotoDisc/Getty Images. 149 (br) © Shutterstock. 150 (b) © Shutterstock. 151A (b) Photodisc/Getty Images. 151A (b) © Getty Images/PhotoDisc. 151A (b) © Frank & Joyce Burek/PhotoDisc/Getty Images. 151B (b) Brand X Pictures/Getty Images. All other images property of HMH Publishers.